Quinceañera

CELEBRATING FIFTEEN

Quinceañera

CELEBRATING FIFTEEN

ELIZABETH KING

Dutton Children's Books · New York

ACKNOWLEDGMENTS

Eduardo, Margarita, Christina, Cindy, and Jason Chávez; Alfonso, Angela, Suzana,
and Gustavo Prieto; the extended families and friends of the *quinceañeras*; the elegant
damas and *chambelanes*; Ana Serrato (Web site: http://clnet.ucr.edu/research/folklore/
quinceaneras); Elva García; Luis Torres Photography; Navarro Fotografía y Video;
Vicki Villaseñor and the staff at El Pueblo Bakery & Panadería; Irma Villanueva; Sylvia
Hernández; Luz Guerrero; Rosa Deras of Cupido's Bridal; Fiesta Mexicana (Mariachi);
Kevin Feeney of the San Fernando Mission; Magdalena Esquivel; Barbara Kuras;
Ethel Nolet; Sheridan Wolfe; Adela Vargas; Martha King; Dale, Taylor,
and Claire Ettema; and Kathleen Minor.

Special thanks to Father Paul Hruby,
who directed me to these wonderful families
and gave generously of his time and faith.

And with much appreciation,
Susan Van Metre of Dutton Children's Books,
editor and friend.

Library of Congress Cataloging-in-Publication Data
KING, ELIZABETH, date.
QUINCEAÑERA: CELEBRATING FIFTEEN / BY ELIZABETH KING—1ST ED.   P.   CM.
SUMMARY: FOCUSES ON DESCRIBING THE CELEBRATION OF THIS RITE
OF PASSAGE IN THE LIVES OF TWO LATINAS, WHILE ALSO PRESENTING
HISTORICAL BACKGROUND FOR THE OCCASION.
ISBN 0-525-45638-4
1. QUINCEAÑERA (SOCIAL CUSTOM)—UNITED STATES—JUVENILE LITERATURE.
2. [1. QUINCEAÑERA (SOCIAL CUSTOM)]   I. TITLE.
GT2490.K56   1998   395.2'4—DC21   97-44539   CIP   AC

PUBLISHED IN THE UNITED STATES 1998
BY DUTTON CHILDREN'S BOOKS,
A MEMBER OF PENGUIN PUTNAM INC.
345 HUDSON STREET, NEW YORK, NEW YORK 10014
DESIGNED BY ELLEN M. LUCAIRE
MANUFACTURED IN CHINA • FIRST EDITION
4   6   8   10   9   7   5

FOR

Cindy Melissa Chávez
&
Suzana Prieto

TO EACH OF YOU . . .

"Hoy, te podemos ver bailar ya tu primer vals."

(FROM *"Quinceañera"* BY ROBERTO BELESTER—AMÉRICA MUSICAL)

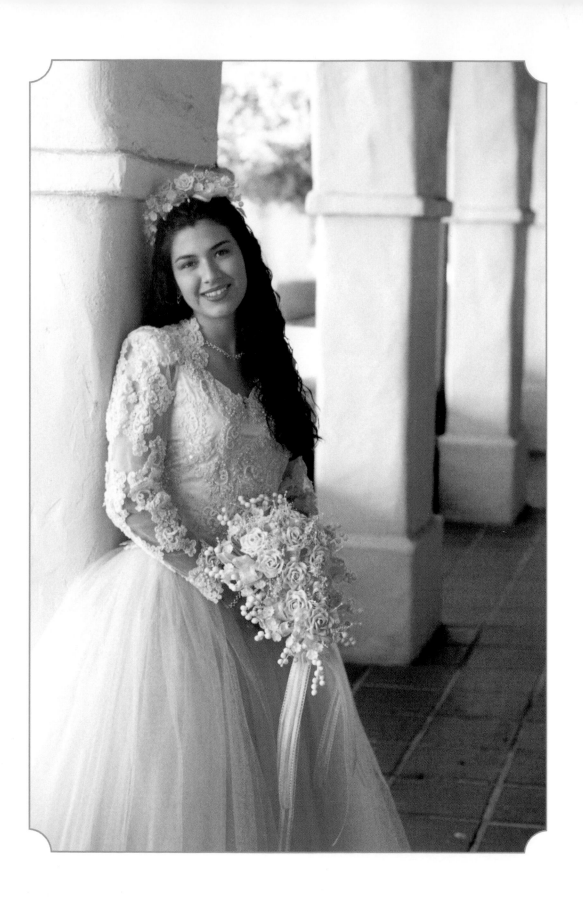

THE DREAM

CINDY MELISSA CHÁVEZ POSES patiently for the photographer. This picture will be one that she and her family treasure forever. Today is Cindy's *quinceañera*—the celebration of her fifteenth birthday. But unlike any of the birthdays that have come before, this one will be celebrated by everyone who knows her with a church ceremony and a big party. Cindy is no longer a little girl to her family and friends, but a young woman.

In the traditions of many groups of people, children are given special attention when they reach a certain birthday—the age when they are recognized as the newest adults in their community. The ceremonies marking these days are called rites of passage, rituals that signify a person is ready to move to a new stage in her life.

Coming-of-age ceremonies serve an important purpose for a society, because they strengthen the bond between a person and her community. Like a wedding, this is a time when promises are made. A young person promises to take on an adult role, and her community promises to support and welcome her when she does. Many young Jewish women have a bat mitzvah, or religious ceremony, when they turn thirteen. They are called to read a portion of the Torah, a sacred scroll containing the five books of Moses and the Jewish code of morals and values. The *nai'es* is an Apache coming-of-age celebration for girls who have reached puberty—they are "danced" into adulthood by their community. And in some parts of the country, teenage girls have debutante parties to mark their entrance into social life.

The *quinceañera* is the way many Latino families acknowledge that a girl has grown up. The word *quinceañera* is used for both the celebration and the girl it honors. The celebration is also known as *quince años*. Translated from Spanish, *quince* means "fifteen" and *años* means "years."

Traditionally, a young Latina was not allowed to dance, go out on dates, or wear makeup before she had her *quinceañera*. Rules have changed, and young women know that there is a lot more to being an adult, but for many Latinas this is still a very important day—one they have dreamed about since childhood.

Though it was not originally a Catholic tradition, the Church views the *quinceañera* celebration as an opportunity for a "teachable moment"—a chance to talk to the young woman about her faith and its importance in her adult life.

In preparation for the big day, Cindy and her parents first visited with Father Paul Hruby at their church. Through the years, Father Paul, a Roman Catholic priest, has guided Cindy's spiritual growth. Father Paul will perform a special Mass for Cindy to give thanks that she has reached her fifteenth year and to reaffirm her faith and dedication to God. He also officiated at Cindy's sister Christina's *quinceañera*. Father Paul, Cindy, and her parents, Eduardo and Margarita Chávez, discuss when the Mass should take place and where. The *quinceañera* doesn't have to take place on Cindy's birthday, but close to it.

They decide to have the Mass at the historical Mission San Fernando Rey de España, better known as the San Fernando Mission in Mission Hills, California. Founded by Father Fermin Lasuén in 1797, the mission was one of twenty-one built along what was called *El Camino Real*, the Royal Highway, along the California coast.

The missions were placed approximately one day's walk from one another. They were begun by Father Junípero Serra at the behest of the Spanish king Charles III in 1769. California was Spanish and Mexican territory before it became part of the United States.

The missions helped strengthen Spain's claim on the land. They were centers of trade and of efforts to convert Native Americans to Catholicism. Many of California's important towns and cities first formed around these mission sites. The San Fernando Mission, with its rich history, seems like a good place for a ceremony about community.

Father Paul and the Chávezes also discuss the biblical passages that will be read during the ceremony. Father Paul tells Cindy that she must take part in confirmation classes first, though her confirmation will be a separate ceremony. These classes will include community service. She and her friends will make meals in the church kitchen for people in need, showing the responsibility they will take as adults for their community's well-being.

Everyone who knows Cindy will want to acknowledge this important change in her status. And there are many things Cindy and her family, friends, and community must do to prepare for the big day. *Quinceañeras* can also be costly. Some parents pay for and plan the entire event, but many others receive gifts or services from their daughter's *padrinos*, her godparents. Cindy has many *padrinos*.

One of the most expensive items is the *vestido*, or dress. Cindy and her mother have visited the dressmaker, Luz Guerrero. She is busy sewing Cindy's *vestido* in her home workshop. She makes many *vestidos* and other clothing for *quinceañeras* and *bodas*, or weddings. Cindy's mother decided to have Luz make Cindy's special *vestido* because she had seen examples of her fine workmanship at other celebrations. Luz is also making the *vestidos* for Cindy's *damas*, or ladies (attendants). Cindy's *chambelanes*, or lords (escorts), will rent tuxedos. Sometimes the escorts are called *caballeros*, or gentlemen.

Cindy's *vestido* will be made of pink satin, organza, lace, and beading. Cindy's family is originally from El Salvador, in Central America. In that country, the *quinceañera* is called Mi *fiesta rosa*, or My Pink Party. The Salvadorans believe that only brides should wear a white *vestido*. But Latinas of Mexican heritage usually wear white for their *quinceañeras*. The *quinceañera* tradition is also strongest in Mexico. It is believed to have originated there and to have come from Aztec customs.

There are other differences in the ways Latino cultures celebrate the *quinceañera*. For instance, many young women in the Cuban culture celebrate with just a ball and no special Mass, but what a ball! They wear lavish dresses and appear in highly rehearsed and choreographed production numbers, sometimes even making an entrance by stepping out of a huge clamshell! And some Latino cultures do not celebrate the *quinceañera* at all.

Not far from Cindy and in the same California valley, Suzana Prieto is also preparing for her *quinceañera*. Her family is originally from Mexico. She is having measurements taken for a beautiful white *vestido*. In the display cases of the storefront shop are other items for *quinceañeras*. One is a *corona*, or crown, made of rhinestones, pearls, or flowers.

Suzana has been looking forward to this day for years. When she was a little girl, she would say to her mother on each of her birthdays, "Mami, I want my *quinceañera*—I want my *quinceañera*!" And then she would eagerly count the years before she would turn fifteen. When she finally did, her parents gave her the option of having a *quinceañera*, going on a trip, or getting a car. Suzi chose the *quinceañera*.

"It is my culture—it is what has been passed down to me. Just hearing about it—to me it is a big deal," says Suzi.

Over the years, Suzi has attended many *quinceañeras*, either as a guest or as a participant. But Suzi is the first girl on both sides of her family to have a *quinceañera*. In Mexico, only the well-to-do could afford the cost of a *quinceañera*, or sometimes the girl chose not to have one.

Another important traditional element of the *quinceañera* is the *pastel*, or cake. One set of Cindy Chávez's godparents has ordered a special *pastel* from El Pueblo Bakery & Panadería.

Inside the bakery and bread store, wonderful smells come from warm Mexican breads of every shape and description. In the kitchen, the bakers make and decorate cakes for all occasions. Saul is making a birthday cake with fruit. Hector, who has been a baker for fourteen years, is making an elaborate wedding cake. The owner, Vicki Villaseñor, puts strings of *perlas*, or pearls, on a layer of the cake. Each cake is eaten the day it is made. Come the Saturday morning of Cindy's *quinceañera*, Hector and the other bakers will be busy as usual, creating a dreamy confection, but this time with pink flowers!

There are precious few weeks before Suzi Prieto's *quinceañera*, and special nights have been set aside for dance rehearsal. The patio lights have been turned on, and Suzi's backyard has become a dance studio. Alfonso, her father, has asked his cousin Irma Villanueva to teach Suzi's *damas* and *chambelanes* the *vals*, or waltz, and other choreographed dances for the party after the Mass. Everybody has a good time, even if some do feel awkward dancing the *vals*. And there's still time to talk with good friends.

It is traditional for a *quinceañera* to be escorted at her ceremony by a group of young people called an honor court, or *corte de honor*. This group of *damas*, ladies, and *chambelanes*, lords, plus the *quinceañera* and her escort make fifteen couples, each couple representing a year of the *quinceañera*'s life. But many families shape the tradition to their wishes or circumstances, making their own unique celebration.

For instance, some *quinceañeras* have only *damas*, some have just *chambelanes*. Others have the whole *corte de honor*. Suzi will have a full honor court. Cindy Chávez will also have a *corte de honor*, but a smaller one.

Both Suzi and Cindy have asked family and friends to be in their *corte*. *Quinceañeras* usually ask their good female friends to be *damas*. The girls then suggest boys to be the *chambelanes*. Traditionally in Mexico, the *damas* and the *chambelanes* must be younger than the *quinceañera*, but Suzi and Cindy will have many friends their own age. Still, they must ask all the parents for permission to include the friends in the festivities. Making arrangements is part of being a grown-up, but the *quinceañera*'s parents usually help with this big task.

The hardest part is picking up the phone to ask someone to be their own escort, the *chambelán de honor*. All of a sudden, the girls experience a serious case of shyness. This special person is usually a school friend, family friend, or relative. Cindy chooses Rurik Madrid, a friend. Suzi asks Jessie Prieto, her cousin.

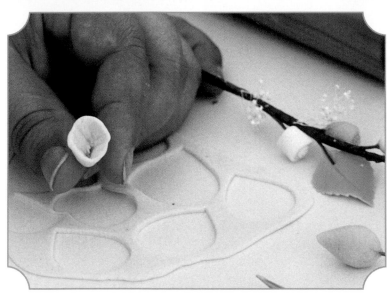

One Saturday afternoon before her *quinceañera*, Cindy visits Sylvia Hernández, one of her mother's friends. Margarita has asked Sylvia to make special *recuerdos*, or mementos, that will be given to each guest at the party. Sylvia makes beautiful flowers from corn dough, a skill she learned in her home country of Mexico. She shapes the colored dough into rose petals, and then into dozens of delicate single roses. The dough remains flexible, even after it has dried, but it keeps for a very long time.

Sylvia makes not only Cindy's *recuerdos*, but also her *ramo*, or bouquet, and her *corona*. Both are pink, of course, to match Cindy's gown. Cindy tries on her *corona* with her regular clothes, and already she is transformed into a queen. Behind her is a *flor de izote*, which is the national flower of El Salvador.

LA QUINCEAÑERA

·•◗●◖•·

IT IS SATURDAY MORNING at the Chávez family apartment. The sunlight streams through the window. In the early light, Cindy's aunt Isabel carefully applies Cindy's makeup. The family has been awake for hours finishing last-minute preparations and anticipating the day. Whatever may befall Cindy in the future, it will never diminish this, her *quinceañera*. Cindy's sister, Christina, has come home from UCLA to be with her on this important day.

Luz has done a wonderful job. Cindy's *vestido* is magnificent! On the bed are some of the other treasures of the day: her *zapatos* (shoes), *libro* (prayer book), and *rosario* (rosary).

The family arrives at the grand Mission San Fernando Rey de España. The mission is made of adobe, or mud and straw, and decorated with beautiful Spanish and Native American designs. The mission has withstood centuries of use and disrepair, even the earthquakes of 1971 and 1994. The church itself crumbled in the 1971 quake, but was rebuilt to authentic specifications. A statue of San Fernando, or Saint Ferdinand, sent by the Spanish king Charles III still stands above the altar.

While waiting for the celebration to begin, Cindy watches the peacocks that live on the mission grounds. Like Cindy, they wear a *corona* on top of their colorful heads. In mission times, peacocks were kept by landowners for their beauty. But even with their jewel-toned feathers, the peacocks can't match Cindy's finery today.

It is time for *la misa*, the Mass, in Cindy's honor. Cindy opens the heavy wooden door of the mission, and the centuries-old celebration begins. A mariachi band plays as Cindy and her *corte de honor* enter the church. Cindy's *padrinos* hired them to play as a gift for the *quinceañera*.

After her beautiful *damas* are escorted into the church by their handsome *chambelanes*, Cindy slowly walks down the aisle with her proud parents. Father Paul awaits at the altar, smiling.

The music ends, and in the silence Father Paul begins to speak—in Spanish. He greets Cindy and the congregation. Next, Cindy's two best friends, Marisela Reyes and Crystal Barragan, read passages from the Bible, specially chosen for this occasion.

Father Paul reads the homily explaining the biblical passages. They speak of the call to God and the role of Mary as a model of faith. On the wall of the old church is a painting of Our Lady of Guadalupe, a dark-complexioned version of the Virgin Mary. Many believe that she appeared to a man named Juan Diego outside Mexico City in 1531. Her image was imprinted on Juan Diego's cloak, and when he showed it to a Catholic bishop, fresh roses fell from it. Our Lady of Guadalupe is an important figure of faith for many Latino Catholics; she is also the patron saint of Mexico.

Father Paul asks that Cindy keep her faith in God, just as Mary did as a young woman when God called upon her to be the mother of Jesus.

Next, the symbolic *quinceañera* gifts are presented to Cindy by her godparents, Salvador and Ana Arévalo. As her *padrino* and *madrina*, they have been there for her baptism, First Communion, and now her *quinceañera*. The gifts are first blessed by Father Paul. The *libro* represents the words that will guide Cindy on her life's journey. The *rosario* is symbolic of the mysteries of salvation, and the ring represents God's love, which, like a circle, has no beginning and no end.

As Cindy listens to the words of Father Paul, she can't help crying. Now she knows why she feels so different today. It is all too much—the realization that her family and friends are together just for her, thanking God that she has reached adulthood.

Father Paul hands Cindy the microphone so she can be heard by all as she makes her prayer of dedication to God. She has memorized it for the occasion.

The Mass proceeds with the Feast of the Holy Eucharist, or Communion. Father Paul begins by blessing the Communion wafer and wine, the body and blood of Christ. Cindy receives the Communion, then her *corte* and the rest of the congregation are invited to join the Holy Feast.

Finally, Cindy is given her *ramo natural*, or fresh bouquet, by her godmother. She places it at the feet of the statue of the Virgin Mary and says a silent prayer.

The mariachis begin to play, signaling the end of the Mass. Now, holding her bouquet made of corn dough, Cindy is warmly embraced by her father and mother. They are so proud. She leaves the church with Rurik Madrid, her *chambelán de honor*, and the rest of her *corte*. They are ready for the party, but first they pose for a few more photographs in the mission garden.

Because of its beauty and historical significance, the San Fernando Mission is a popular place for *quinceañera* observances. Suzi Prieto is having hers there, also. But Suzi's Mexican heritage and her own personal style mean that her ceremony will be different from Cindy's.

Suzi wears a beautiful traditional white *vestido* and has a matching heart-shaped *cojín* made by her mother, Angela. When Suzi speaks and reaffirms her dedication to her faith, it is apparent that she has had a lot of experience with the public. She works part-time as a receptionist at her local church, so she knows how to talk comfortably with people and to help solve problems. Father Paul notes the active role that Suzi plays in her community and the good feelings everyone has for her. Suzi plans to work with people in the future, too—she wants to be a pediatrician.

In a touching moment during the ceremony, Suzi's father places the *corona* on his daughter's head. It is wonderful to be queen for the day.

Outside the church, there are smiles all around. Suzi's little nephew looks sharp in his pint-sized tuxedo.

La fiesta

❖

Cindy's friends and family have spent hours decorating the local women's club hall for the party. There are balloons, ribbons, and colored teddy bears that match the dresses of each of the *damas*. Off to the side, on a special table of its own, is Cindy's *pastel*. It has seven tiers and a real running fountain! Figurines of the *corte de honor* ascend a stairway, and a little *muñeca*, or doll, representing Cindy crowns the *pastel*.

Cindy and her mother hand out the *recuerdos* to every guest. Attached are ribbons that read: "*Recuerdo de Mis XV, 28 October 1995, Cindy M. Chávez*" (In honor of my fifteen years, October 28, 1995, Cindy M. Chávez). These will be saved by all the guests and placed inside their fine-china cabinets, next to the *recuerdos* of other important occasions.

The *damas* and *chambelanes* talk and laugh easily with one another. Some have been friends for years. With coiffed hair, makeup, and elaborate dresses, the girls look elegant, but they can still be silly.

Dinner is served buffet style. Eduardo and Margarita have chosen to offer their guests beef and chicken fajitas, or strips of meat with onions, peppers, and tomatoes wrapped in soft tortillas, and *cóctel de camarones*, or shrimp cocktail, made with shrimp, tomato sauce, chiles, cilantro, onion, and lemon.

While the guests are eating, the DJ plays lots of different styles of music. There is something for everyone: salsa, merengue, *cumbia*, *romántico*, old school, techno, and deep house.

When the dinner is over, guests sing "*Las mañanitas*," a Mexican serenade that is also a birthday song. Cindy's father addresses their guests and makes *un brindis*, a toast, to Cindy and her future happiness. The guests raise their special *copas*, or glasses, filled with sparkling apple juice. Then they drink to Cindy, the *quinceañera*.

The *corte de honor* goes backstage for a last-minute dance rehearsal. The waltz music begins, and Cindy and her father promenade (*pasean*) around the floor, waving to the guests. They dance alone. A new waltz begins, and Cindy turns to dance with Rurik, her escort. Then the rest of the *corte de honor* join the couple in a waltz. All the practicing has paid off, and the couples glide across the floor effortlessly. The grand sweep of their arms and the colorful twirls of their dresses catch the lights. On the sidelines, two little girls watch the fairy-tale scene and imagine their own *quinceañeras*.

At the fiesta for Suzi Prieto, a young girl signs the guest book. Next to it is a *muñeca* and a framed picture of Suzi when she was a little girl. The *muñeca* represents *el último juguete*, the last toy, and Suzi will give it away to one of the younger people at the party.

A friend of Suzi's parents has prepared a very special dish that is made for celebrations in Mexico and now in the United States. It is called *birria*. It is a dish that is traditionally made with a whole *chivo*, or goat, that has been freshly killed and then marinated in meat juice, tomatoes, chiles, and spices. It is then steamed in an oven overnight. If prepared correctly, it is *delicioso*, delicious.

A mariachi band plays as Suzi throws the *muñeca* up in the air for one of her young friends to catch. It is time for Suzi to dance a waltz with her father, but first he kneels at her feet and changes her "little girl" patent-leather shoes for a young lady's high-heeled *zapatos*.

Her mother and the other guests laugh appreciatively as her father struggles with the task. It's the first time Suzi has worn heels. Traditionally, this act marked the beginning of a young woman's social life. She was then allowed to be courted by eligible suitors.

Both fiestas last long into the night as family and friends celebrate Cindy Chávez and Suzana Prieto. Each has entered a new phase of her young life—and in the words of señor Eduardo Chávez to his daughter Cindy:

"Qué fascinador es tener una hija como tú, y en este día tan inolvidable, que dejas de ser una niña para convertirte en mujer, déjame expresarte lo orgulloso que nos sentimos de ti, que la vida siempre te sonría, que tus sueños se hagan realidad y que tus ilusiones esten siempre llenas de esa blanca e inocente candidez que te caracteriza . . . Muchas felicidades, hija. Tu papi, tu mami, tu hermana y tu hermano."

"It is fascinating to have a daughter like you, and today, a memorable day, when you become a woman, let me express how much we are proud of you. May life always smile on you, that all your dreams may come true, and that your hopes and expectations may always be full of that white and innocent candidness that characterizes you. . . . Happy birthday, Cindy, from your dad, your mom, your sister, and your brother."

THE ORIGINS

———— ◆●◆ ————

WHEN DID PEOPLE FIRST celebrate *quinceañeras*? It is difficult to be sure, but puberty marked a time of social change for Aztec girls in pre-Columbian Central America. The *Codex Mendoza*, a history of Aztec customs written in the sixteenth century by native peoples of Mexico, describes the Aztec girl's education. A mother instructed her daughter when she was young. She taught her how to grind corn into meal, spin cotton, and weave fabrics on the loom. But when the girl reached a certain birthday, she might be sent to one of two types of schools.

Daughters of nobles went to a school called a *calmecac*, where they were taught by priestesses, preparing for a life of religious service or for marriage. The *calmecac* was an austere place. The girls were expected to live chastely, take part in religious rituals, embroider fine materials, and make several nightly offerings of incense to the gods.

Daughters of commoners typically went to a less formal school called a *telpochcalli*. They were taught by women called *ichpochtlatoque*, "mistresses of the girls," and usually left school for marriage.

By the time she was fifteen, an Aztec girl was considered ready to leave her parents' and teachers' care and to take on her adult role as a priestess or wife. The coming-of-age rituals were adapted after the arrival of the Spanish and the Catholic Church in Central America. When the Austrian Maximilian and his wife, Carlota, were made emperor and empress of Mexico in the nineteenth century, they brought a lavish style to celebrations. Waltz music written by fellow Austrian Johann Strauss, ball gowns, and dancing were a part of social life at their court. Bridging time and culture, the great traditions of Europe and the Americas combined and shaped the way in which the *quinceañera* is celebrated by young women today.